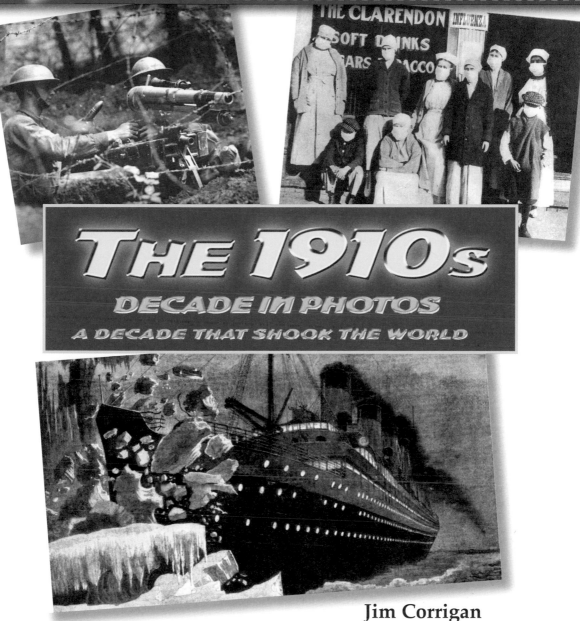

THE 1910s
DECADE IN PHOTOS
A DECADE THAT SHOOK THE WORLD

Jim Corrigan

Enslow Publishers, Inc.
40 Industrial Road
Box 398
Berkeley Heights, NJ 07922
USA

http://www.enslow.com

Library of Congress Cataloging-in-Publication Data

Corrigan, Jim.
  The 1910s decade in photos: a decade that shook the world / by Jim Corrigan.
    p. cm. — (Amazing decades in photos)
  Includes bibliographical references and index.
  Summary: "Middle school readers will find out about the important world, national, and cultural
developments of the decade 1910–1919"—Provided by publisher.
  ISBN-13: 978-0-7660-3130-2
  ISBN-10: 0-7660-3130-6
  1. History, Modern—20th century—Pictorial works—Juvenile literature. 2. Nineteen tens—
Pictorial works—Juvenile literature. I. Title. II. Title: Nineteen tens decade in photos.
  E756.C79 2009
  973.91'3—dc22

                                                    2008042902

Printed in the United States of America.

092009 Lake Book Manufacturing, Inc., Melrose Park, IL

10 9 8 7 6 5 4 3 2 1

To Our Readers: We have done our best to make sure all Internet Addresses in this book were active and appropriate when we went to press. However, the author and the publisher have no control over and assume no liability for the material available on those Internet sites or on other Web sites they may link to. Any comments or suggestions can be sent by email to comments@enslow.com or to the address on the back cover.

Every effort has been made to locate all copyright holders of material used in this book. If any errors or omissions have occurred, corrections will be made in future editions of this book.

♻ Enslow Publishers, Inc., is committed to printing our books on recycled paper. The paper in every book contains 10% to 30% post-consumer waste (PCW). The cover board on the outside of each book contains 100% PCW. Our goal is to do our part to help young people and the environment too!

Produced by OTTN Publishing, Stockton, N.J.

TABLE OF CONTENTS

WELCOME TO THE 1910s

Progress does not mean the end of problems—that was the lesson of the 1910s. People had made great gains during the first decade of the twentieth century. They saw many advances in science and technology. This progress would continue during the 1910s. However, there would also be many terrible disasters during this decade. These slowed society's zeal for rapid growth. By the end of the decade, many people longed for a simpler time.

Some of the disasters during the 1910s showed that science and technology did not hold all of the answers. One example was the sinking of *Titanic* in April 1912. The ocean liner was considered a modern marvel. Many people

Composer and songwriter Irving Berlin (1888–1989) became nationally famous in 1911 for his first hit, "Alexander's Ragtime Band." Berlin would go on to write hundreds of popular songs, including "God Bless America" in 1918.

This famous poster from 1917 encouraged Americans to join the army and go overseas to fight during World War I. The conflict had started in Europe during August 1914, but the fighting soon spread to other continents. At first the United States did not want to get involved. However, in April 1917, the U.S. declared war on Germany and its allies.

SUCCESSFULLY INTRUDUCED BY EMMA CARUS

ALEXANDER'S RAGTIME BAND

BY IRVING BERLIN ~

In the late nineteenth and early twentieth centuries, a new idea emerged that changed life in the United States. This idea was called progressivism. Progressivism sought to fix the problems that America faced as it became a major industrial nation, such as poverty and terrible working conditions. Progressive reformers like Jane Addams developed the concept of "social workers"—people who were trained to help those in need. During the 1910s, progressives fought for shorter hours, better wages, and safer conditions for workers. They also tried to enact laws prohibiting child labor.

thought *Titanic* was unsinkable—until, shockingly, it went down after colliding with an iceberg.

Later in the decade, a flu epidemic spread across the globe. It brought sickness and death. All the advances of modern medicine could not stop a tiny virus from causing an illness that killed millions of people.

Science and technology were not always applied in peaceful or benevolent ways, either. New factories created modern weapons that made it easier to kill. The machine gun could fire six hundred bullets per minute. A tank could destroy everything in its path. Poison gases could blind a soldier's eyes and burn his lungs. In August 1914, these terrifying weapons were unleashed. Millions of soldiers used them in World War I.

World War I was the worst tragedy of the 1910s. It killed ten million people. At first, Americans wanted nothing to do with the war. They felt it was strictly a matter involving European countries, like Great Britain, Germany, France, and Russia. But the war affected the United States. A new weapon called the submarine roamed the seas. German submarine attacks on ships claimed many American victims. Eventually, the nation and its president chose to fight.

American soldiers entered the First World War in 1917. They fought on the side of Great Britain, France, and other countries, known as the Allies. Their enemies were Germany, Austria-Hungary, and their allies, called the Central powers. America helped the Allies win the war.

U.S. president Woodrow Wilson proposed a peace plan that would be fair to all. However, the other Allies refused. They wanted to punish their enemies for the war. The Allies also wanted to build up their own empires. They forced Germany and the Central powers to give up some of their land. The defeated countries also had to agree to pay the Allies a huge amount of money.

Americans thought they had made the world a safer and more peaceful place. They were wrong. People in the defeated nations were bitter about the treaty. Without realizing it, the treaty's authors had sown the seeds for another world war.

American soldiers returned from the battlefield to find that important changes were taking place at home. Throughout the 1910s, women tried to earn the right to vote. Americans approved the Seventeenth Amendment to the U.S. Constitution, which allowed senators to be elected by the people. This was considered a major progressive accomplishment. Many immigrants arrived from other countries. They wanted to become U.S. citizens. Good things were happening in the United States. A young film industry took root in Hollywood, California. By the end of 1919, Americans did not want to hear any more about wars or bad news from overseas. After a decade of disasters, Americans were ready to have some fun.

A group of immigrants wait in a line as they depart their ship at Ellis Island, New York. Between 1910 and 1919, more than 6.3 million immigrants came to the United States looking for a better life.

Titanic collides with an iceberg late on the evening of April 14, 1912. More than 1,500 people were killed when the enormous ocean liner sank in the North Atlantic.

TITANIC TRAGEDY SHOCKS THE WORLD

People said *Titanic* was a marvel. It was the biggest ship of its time. It was unsinkable, they said. They were wrong. *Titanic* would hit an iceberg on its very first voyage. The results would be tragic.

   Titanic was a British ocean liner. The ship was built to carry people across the Atlantic Ocean in style and comfort. The gleaming ship was longer than a city block. It had nine decks and could carry more than 3,500 people.

A photo of *Titanic* taken in 1912. The first trip taken by a ship, aircraft, or other craft is sometimes called the "maiden voyage."

Though large, it could move across the water quickly. *Titanic* set off on its first voyage on April 10, 1912. It left from Southampton, England. Many famous and wealthy people were aboard. They stayed in beautiful cabins. They enjoyed tasty food. Poor people also traveled on *Titanic*. Although their rooms and meals were not as luxurious, they were excited to be on such a wonderful ship.

The first few days of the journey to New York were quiet. Guests enjoyed the comforts of the beautiful new ocean liner. Nobody knew that disaster lay ahead. Icebergs pose a threat to ships sailing in the North Atlantic. The huge chunks of ice can damage a ship. They can also be difficult to see at night.

Just before midnight on April 14, 1912, *Titanic* struck an iceberg. The ship began taking on water. At first, the crew did not realize how badly *Titanic* was damaged. The iceberg had torn long gashes in the side of the ship. *Titanic* had been built to withstand some damage, but not this much. The ship was sinking.

The *New York Herald* on April 15, 1912, announces news of the sinking. The story contained few details, as the *Carpathia* did not arrive in New York with the survivors until April 18. Pictured on the newspaper's front page are some of the famous and wealthy passengers who died when the ship went down. They included John Jacob Astor, a wealthy real estate tycoon; Isidor Straus, the co-owner of Macy's department store in New York; and William T. Stead, a British journalist and reformer.

The rust-covered bow of *Titanic*, photographed in 2004. The remains of the doomed ocean liner were rediscovered in 1985 by oceanographer Robert Ballard. *Titanic* lies two and a half miles below the surface of the Atlantic Ocean. Recent studies indicate that the ship is deteriorating rapidly.

The captain gave the order to abandon ship, but the process went slowly. Many guests were still asleep. They had to be woken up and led to lifeboats. Even worse, *Titanic* did not have enough lifeboats. There was only enough room on the lifeboats for about half of the passengers on the ship.

The ship sank in less than three hours. More than 1,500 people plunged into the icy water. Most quickly froze to death. Some of the victims were millionaires. Others were immigrants hoping for a better life in America.

The *Titanic* tragedy led to a number of safety reforms. New laws required lifeboat space for all passengers on a ship. The International Ice Patrol was formed to spot dangerous icebergs. New methods were developed for rescue at sea. The sinking of *Titanic* proved to the world that no machine was perfect.

SCOUTING IS ESTABLISHED IN THE UNITED STATES

Lord Robert Baden-Powell (1857–1941) is considered the founder of Scouting.

In 1909, a wealthy American named W.D. Boyce was visiting London. While walking through the city, he became lost. A young boy helped him back to his hotel. Boyce offered a tip, but the boy refused. He explained that he was a Boy Scout and had to do a good deed every day. Impressed, Boyce decided to learn more about Scouting.

A British Army general named Robert Baden-Powell had started the Boy Scout program in Great Britain. The purpose of Scouting was to help young men become productive

Boy Scouts swim at a camp in New York, circa 1919. Today, nearly eight million young Americans are members of the Boy Scouts or Girl Scouts. Many former Scouts have become very successful as adults. Presidents who had once been Boy Scouts include John F. Kennedy, Gerald Ford, and Bill Clinton.

This 1917 poster features a Boy Scout encouraging Americans to buy Liberty Bonds. The Scout is holding a sword engraved with the organization's motto, "Be Prepared." Liberty Bonds were used to help pay for American involvement in World War I.

members of society. In 1908, Baden-Powell wrote a book called *Scouting for Boys.* It was used as a guide for the program.

When Boyce returned to America, he met with other people interested in teaching boys useful social skills. One was Ernest Thompson Seton, who had founded a group called the Woodland Scouts in 1902. Another was Daniel Carter Beard, who had started the Sons of Daniel Boone in 1905. In 1910, the Boy Scouts of America was established. The Woodland Scouts, Sons of Daniel Boone, and several other youth groups became part of the Boy Scouts.

Scout troops were soon started in many American cities and towns. At first, the program was open to boys between the ages of eleven and sixteen. Outdoor activities, such as camping and hiking, were used to teach boys how to be self-reliant and resourceful. Troop leaders tried to show Scouts how to be good citizens who helped others. The Boy Scout program was so popular that a similar organization, the Girl Scouts of the United States of America, was created in 1912.

Juliette Gordon Low, founder of the Girl Scouts, is on the right in this 1917 photo of the first Girl Scout troop's leaders. Low (1860–1927) based the Girl Scouts on a British organization, the Girl Guides. Lord Robert Baden-Powell and his wife, Olave, had started the Girl Guides program.

IMMIGRANTS ARRIVE IN RECORD NUMBERS

Young Italian immigrants work as street vendors in Indianapolis, circa 1910.

People who move from one country to another are called immigrants. The United States has always attracted many immigrants. They come to America seeking a new and better life. In the 1910s, record numbers of immigrants came to America.

From 1892 to 1954, Ellis Island was the main entry point for immigrants coming to the United States. More than 12 million immigrants were processed at this facility in New York harbor. Today, more than 100 million Americans can trace their roots back to an ancestor who entered the country through Ellis Island.

From 1880 to 1914, more than 22 million immigrants set foot on America's shores. The country had never before seen so many newcomers. The new arrivals found jobs and worked hard. They made America stronger. They also brought new ideas and traditions from their native lands.

Not everyone was happy about this. There was tension between immigrants and people who had been born in America. Some Americans feared that newcomers would take their jobs or homes. Others did not like the languages, traditions, and religious beliefs of the immigrants.

Since the 1880s, Congress had restricted the flow of new immigrants from certain areas, such as China and Japan. In 1917, a new law reduced the total number of immigrants allowed to come to America. Future laws passed in the 1920s would basically end all new immigration to America until the mid-1960s. Today, some people are still concerned about the effect of immigration on American society.

Members of a Polish immigrant family work on a farm near Baltimore. Most of the immigrants who came to the United States between 1890 and 1917 were from southern and eastern Europe. When these immigrants arrived in the United Sates, they often encountered prejudice because of their different customs, languages, and religious beliefs.

PAYING INCOME TAX

By the 1910s, the United States had become a major world power. But as America's economic and military strength increased, so did the cost of running its government. The services that a national, or federal, government provides can be very costly. These services include building roads, feeding an army, and running the courts. To pay for these things, the federal government collects taxes from its citizens.

In 1913, Congress passed the Sixteenth Amendment to the Constitution. This amendment allowed the U.S. government to collect income taxes. An income tax is based on the money that people earn from work and other sources. The government created what is called a graduated income tax, because the rate of taxation is divided into regular stages or levels. People who earn more money are at a higher level, and therefore pay more in taxes. People who earn less money are at a lower level, and pay less income tax.

In 1909, President William Howard Taft asked Congress to consider a constitutional amendment allowing the federal government to tax income. Once Congress approved the Sixteenth Amendment, it was sent to the states for ratification.

Amendments to the U.S. Constitution take effect when they have been ratified, or approved, by three-quarters of the states. The Sixteenth Amendment was ratified on February 3, 1913, when New Mexico became the thirty-sixth of the forty-eight states to approve the measure.

Prior to 1913, the U.S. government had collected revenue in other ways. These included property taxes and tariffs. A property tax is based on the value of a citizen's possessions, such as land. A tariff is a tax on products that come from other countries. Many Americans were glad to see the change to an income tax. They viewed it as a fair method of paying for government services, especially since the country expected the federal government to do more. Because most people have an income, they all share in the burden together.

Some Americans opposed the progressive income tax. They argued that high tax rates were not fair to the wealthy. They also said that taxes would stop rich people from investing in business ventures. The income tax still has its critics today.

This political cartoon from 1913 is titled "In safe waters at last." It reflects the opinion that income taxes will benefit the American people.

HOLLYWOOD PRODUCES FEATURE FILMS

Movies were still a new invention in the 1910s. However, by the end of the decade, filmmaking would become a big business.

The very first film studios were located in Europe. However, the U.S. film industry grew quickly in the early twentieth century. American filmmakers like Cecil B. DeMille, D.W. Griffith, and Edwin Porter were pioneers. By the 1910s, Americans had become regular moviegoers.

D.W. Griffith (1875–1948) was one of the most important early American film directors. He directed the first movie filmed in Hollywood, a ten-minute-long silent film titled *In Old California* (1910). Griffith's greatest success came in 1915, with *The Birth of a Nation*. This film was incredibly popular, although it was criticized for its unfavorable portrayal of African Americans.

The first U.S. studios were located in or around New York City. However, this was a difficult place to make movies. The harsh New York winters made it impossible to film outside. In 1910, a studio called the Biograph Company sent a film crew to southern California to shoot a movie during the winter. The Los Angeles area offered fair weather year round. The filmmakers found it ideal for shooting. There were sunny skies and beautiful scenery.

Soon other movie studios were moving from the East Coast to California. Most chose to relocate in a small town called Hollywood, near Los Angeles. It quickly grew into a busy community. By the end of the 1910s, Hollywood dominated the American and world film industries.

Poster for a 1913 Biograph movie called *Three Friends*. The film starred Lionel Barrymore and Mary Pickford. Biograph was one of the first companies to establish a movie studio in Hollywood.

Today, the Hollywood sign remains an easily recognized symbol of the American film industry.

THE VETERAN'S FAREWELL.

"Good Bye, my lad,
I only wish I were young enough
to go with you!"

ENLIST NOW!

THE GREAT WAR BEGINS

A new type of war erupted during the 1910s. It was much larger than any conflict that came before it. Terrifying new weapons made it more deadly than any prior war. Today, we know it as World War I. In the 1910s, people simply called it the Great War.

The problems that caused World War I began many years earlier. In the nineteenth century, the nations of Europe dominated the world. These countries included Britain, France, and Russia. Each controlled distant lands and had used their power to build an empire. The United States also controlled distant lands, but Americans were uncomfortable with the idea of imperial conquest and war. Americans definitely wanted to avoid the conflicts that affected the European empires.

Germany was a newcomer to empire-building. Germany's emperor, Wilhelm II, was eager to expand his empire quickly. To do so, Wilhelm built a huge army and navy. The other nations of Europe grew concerned. They too built up their military forces. Soon the continent brimmed with armed forces that were ready to fight. It was a dangerous situation. Any incident could spark a major conflict.

In June 1914, a crisis developed. It began in the Balkan Peninsula, an area of southeastern Europe. Countries on the peninsula like Serbia, Bulgaria, and Greece had begun fighting in 1912 to gain territory from the nearby Ottoman Empire. Leaders of the Austro-Hungarian Empire, which bordered the Balkans in central Europe, were afraid that Serbia would move into Bosnia-Herzegovina, a territory they controlled. On June 28, 1914, a member of the

This British recruiting poster from 1914 reflects the attitudes of many Europeans at the start of World War I. The prospect of conflict was seen as exciting and patriotic—an opportunity for young people to serve their country. However, the grim reality of modern warfare soon wiped away such romantic ideas.

Empires in 1914
- Britain
- France
- Germany
- Russia
- Austria-Hungary
- Ottoman
- Under British protection or influence
- • Capitals of the Empires

0 — Miles — 2,000

By the early twentieth century, European countries dominated the globe. The British Empire alone covered about one-quarter of earth's land area. Germany's desire to build its own empire was a major cause of World War I.

Austro-Hungarian royal family was shot and killed in Bosnia. His name was Archduke Franz Ferdinand. The murderers were Serbians.

Following his death, events in Europe quickly spun out of control. Austria-Hungary threatened to attack Serbia. Europe's other Great Powers—France, Russia, Germany, and Great Britain—tried to prevent a war. However, Britain, France, and Russia had treaties that required them to support Serbia. Germany was bound by treaty to support Austria-Hungary, and so was the Ottoman Empire. Each country put its army on alert. Countries told each other to stop preparing for war. However, nobody would back down. Early in August 1914, Germany declared war on Russia and France. Soon, the fighting began.

The warring nations were divided into two opposing groups—the Allied powers and the Central powers. The major Allies included Britain, France, Belgium, Serbia, Montenegro, Russia, Italy, and Japan. The Central powers included Germany, Austria-Hungary, Bulgaria, and the Ottoman Empire. Other countries would enter the war later, including the United States.

People soon realized that this new war was different from those of the past. Modern weapons such as the machine gun could kill like never before. Soldiers dug holes to hide from the bullets. These holes soon became deep trenches that ran for hundreds of miles. There were other dangers too, such as bombs and poison gas. Sickness spread through the filthy trenches. A typical battle would involve thousands of soldiers dying to gain a few feet of ground. Nations were shocked by the death and misery they had created. But it was too late. World War I would drag on for more than four years. Millions would die.

A French magazine illustration from June 1914 depicts the assassination of Austrian Archduke Franz Ferdinand in Bosnia. This killing caused an international crisis that would lead Europe to war.

French soldiers handle a machine gun in a trench on the Western Front.

AMERICANS DIE IN LUSITANIA SINKING

The United States was neutral at the start of World War I. That means it did not take sides. President Wilson and most Americans wanted to stay out of the war. They viewed the conflict as European empires fighting for more power. However, staying out of the war proved more difficult than they imagined.

America was not fighting, but it did trade with the Allies. The United States did not intend to favor the Allies over the Central powers at the beginning of

A crowd of people watches the *Lusitania* arrive in New York harbor on the ship's maiden voyage in 1907. The British ocean liner was one of the fastest ships of its day. It was traveling from New York to Liverpool, England, when it was torpedoed in 1915.

A German submarine, called a U-boat, rides through a rough sea. During World War I, the German navy used its U-boats to try to prevent cargo ships from reaching its enemies, Great Britain and France.

the war. Historically, though, American companies had been more likely to do business with Britain and France than with Germany and its allies. As a result, U.S. food and supplies fueled the Allied war effort. Britain, in particular, depended on U.S. goods for its survival.

Ships carried the cargo across the Atlantic Ocean. Germany wanted to stop this flow of food and supplies to its enemy. German submarines, known as U-boats, sailed into the North Atlantic. They had orders to sink any ship that might be carrying war supplies.

The *Lusitania* was a British ocean liner. It was carrying civilian passengers to England, along with military supplies. On May 17, 1915, *Lusitania* was steaming off the coast of Ireland. A German torpedo suddenly slammed into its hull. The broken ship sank in just eighteen minutes. Nearly 1,200 people died, including more than 120 Americans. The sinking outraged many Americans. President Woodrow Wilson warned Germany that further attacks on U.S. citizens would not be tolerated. However, Wilson still wanted to keep America out of the war.

A British propaganda poster encourages Irishmen to join the British army and avenge the *Lusitania* sinking. International anger about the incident caused Germany to stop attacking neutral ships. In early 1917, however, Germany resumed its unrestricted submarine warfare. When three American merchant ships were sunk as a result, the United States declared war on Germany.

Americans Die in *Lusitania* Sinking

U.S. Troops Pursue Pancho Villa

The 1910s also saw civil war in Mexico. Different groups were fighting for control of the country. America watched the Mexican Revolution carefully. If the fighting spilled across the border, U.S. troops would have to get involved.

That is exactly what happened on March 9, 1916. The forces of Mexican rebel leader Francisco "Pancho" Villa crossed the border into New Mexico. Villa was angry because the U.S. government had supported his rival in Mexico. Villa's men raided the small town of Columbus, New Mexico. They killed eighteen people.

The American army's search for Pancho Villa became known as the "Punitive Expedition." This is because the military action was meant to punish the Mexican rebel leader for his 1916 raid into the United States.

Pancho Villa (second from left) with several of his officers. Americans considered Villa (1878–1923) a bandit because his men often robbed others to pay for their fight against the government.

Villa's raid angered President Woodrow Wilson. He sent ten thousand U.S. soldiers, commanded by General John J. Pershing, into Mexico. Their job was to track down and capture Villa. The troops spent nearly a year chasing him through northern Mexico. The United States sent several other armies into Mexico during these years. Among the American soldiers were two young officers. Their names were George S. Patton and Douglas MacArthur. Years later, they would become famous American generals.

The U.S. troops failed to capture Pancho Villa. The border raids continued. However, the Americans did help weaken Villa's ability to fight. By 1920, he was no longer a threat on either side of the border.

American and Mexican soldiers worked together in Mexico during the Punitive Expedition, April 1916.

U.S. Troops Pursue Pancho Villa

JAZZ SOOTHES THE NATION

A new type of music became popular in the 1910s. It was called jazz. African-American musicians invented jazz in the South. The southern city of New Orleans became a center of jazz music.

Early jazz bands used a variety of instruments. The trumpet, violin, and clarinet were some common examples. The new music was lively, and people often danced to it. The musicians often added their own personal style to songs. This was called improvisation. A band leader named Buddy Bolden was one of

This photo shows the distinctive architecture of the French Quarter in New Orleans, Louisiana. Jazz music is believed to have originated in small nightclubs near this area during the early years of the twentieth century.

Sheet music for an early jazz song, published around 1919. Jazz was influenced by several earlier types of music, such as blues, ragtime, and gospel.

the first jazz musicians to add his own style to the new form of jazz music.

After the 1910s, many jazz musicians moved from New Orleans to Chicago. This was part of a larger movement of African Americans from the South to the North. In Chicago, the jazz movement continued to grow. Eventually, jazz became a national form of music enjoyed by millions.

THE GREAT SATCHMO

Louis Armstrong was a brilliant trumpet player. He helped make early jazz music popular. Armstrong was born in New Orleans in 1901. By the time he was eighteen years old, he was thrilling audiences with his musical ability.

Armstrong was a master of improvisation. He created exciting new sounds with his trumpet. In later years, he also used his powerful voice. Armstrong was among the first to use "scat singing." With scat singing, he would insert silly sounds and syllables, such as "razzamatazz-bee-bop," into the song. Sometimes he simply imitated the sound of an instrument.

Louis Armstrong's nickname was Satchmo. It was short for "satchel-mouth," referring to his large mouth. He remained a premier American performer until his death.

Louis Armstrong (1901–1971) was born in New Orleans. He started playing with local jazz bands as a teenager.

AMERICA ENTERS WORLD WAR I

In 1917, President Wilson still hoped to avoid the war raging in Europe. Many other Americans felt the same way. Americans had a variety of reasons for wishing to remain neutral. For some, it had to do with family. People whose parents or grandparents had emigrated

The "Zimmerman Telegram" was a coded message from German foreign minister Arthur Zimmerman to a Mexican official. In the January 16, 1917, telegram, Zimmerman asked for Mexico's help if the United States declared war on Germany. In return, the German government offered to help Mexico regain territory in the American Southwest—the states of New Mexico, Texas, and Arizona. The British intercepted the message, deciphered the code, and gave it to President Wilson. The American public was outraged when it learned about the Zimmerman Telegram.

President Wilson speaks to Congress, announcing that the United States is breaking off relations with Germany. Wilson took this action when Germany resumed its submarine attacks on neutral ships.

American recruits train with bayonets at Fort Worth, Texas. The United States entered the war as an "associated power." This meant that although U.S. troops fought with the Allies in Europe, the Americans were not placed under control of the Allied supreme commander.

from Germany did not wish to fight against Germany. Many other Americans simply had no interest in the war. They felt that it was a European matter, and not worth the loss of American lives.

But Wilson began to rethink America's neutral position. He thought that if the United States did enter the war, it could help end the conflict quickly. Then the United States could shape the postwar world to make it peaceful.

A turning point came in early 1917. British agents intercepted a secret message. It was meant for Germany's ambassador to Mexico. It told the German ambassador to seek a Mexican alliance against the United States. At nearly the same time, German U-boats sank several U.S. cargo ships, causing many American deaths. Americans were outraged.

Congress declared war on April 6, 1917. America joined the Allies in their fight against the Central powers. U.S. troops began preparing to go overseas.

In this poster, the storm of war brews behind a sleeping woman who represents the United States. The patriotic 1917 illustration encouraged all Americans to do their part for the war effort. "Wake Up, America" was created by James M. Flagg, the artist who also created the famous Uncle Sam poster pictured on page 4.

America Enters World War I

Angry workers storm the Winter Palace in St. Petersburg, Russia, in October 1917. The palace was the headquarters for a temporary, or provisional, government that had been created when Tsar Nicholas II gave up power seven months earlier. The Communist workers, who called themselves Bolsheviks, took over the government.

REVOLUTION IN RUSSIA

The nation of Russia was torn by unrest and violence during the 1910s. Russia had been ruled by kings known as tsars (pronounced *zärs*) for hundreds of years. Tsar Nicholas II, who came to power in 1894, was a harsh ruler. Most of his people were poor, but Nicholas II did not care. His attitude, plus other problems in Russia, would cause several uprisings during his reign. Russians took to the streets and demanded change. The most important of these uprisings occurred in 1917. It would become known as the Russian Revolution.

Russians protest against the tsar's government, January 1917. When the tsar abdicated, or gave up power, a provisional government was formed in St. Petersburg. However, the new government soon became unpopular. Russians turned against the provisional government when it did not withdraw from World War I.

World War I was one of Russia's many problems. The nation was not prepared to fight a modern war. Other countries had many factories to make bombs and guns. There were few modern factories in Russia. As a result, Russian soldiers went to war with obsolete, or old-fashioned, weapons. Many Russians were killed or injured. The battlefield losses made people at home sad and upset. The Russian people blamed the tsar for how badly the war was going for the nation.

People also grew angry about their poor living conditions. Russians worked long hours, but had little food or money. Eight out of ten Russians lived in poverty. As the war dragged on, life became harder for the poor people of Russia. Again, they felt Nicholas II was to blame. Yet the tsar showed little concern for their troubles. The mood of the country became very tense.

The bad feelings reached their highest point in 1917. Hundreds of thousands of Russian workers went on strike. They refused to do any more work until they received higher pay and better working conditions. The tsar refused. He sent in troops to attack the striking workers. However, most soldiers agreed with the strikers and joined their cause. Nicholas II realized he had lost control. He stepped down from power on March 15, 1917.

The striking workers rallied around popular leaders such as Vladimir Lenin and Leon Trotsky. These men proposed that Russians replace the rule of the tsars with a Communist form of government. Under Communism, all land and money

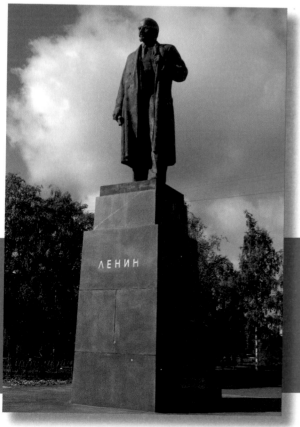

Bolshevik leader Vladimir Lenin (1870–1924) directed the overthrow of Russia's provisional government in October 1917. As head of Russia's Communist government, Lenin defeated the White Army during the civil war. After this, he became the first premier, or leader, of the Soviet Union.

Lenin moved the communist government of Russia to the Kremlin, a palace in Moscow, in March 1918. Since then, the Kremlin has served as the center of Russia's government.

are supposed to be shared equally. All citizens are supposed to work together for the common good. This idea greatly appealed to Russia's many poor people.

A Communist government took control in October 1917. Vladimir Lenin was its leader. The new government soon withdrew Russia from World War I. Russia signed a peace treaty with the Central powers. In the treaty, the Communists gave up control of some territories that had once been part of the Russian Empire. These lands included Finland, Latvia, Lithuania, Poland, and Ukraine.

Not all Russians supported the Communist government. Russians who owned land, for example, did not want to give up their property to the Communist state. Other people wanted to see Russia become a democracy like the United States. In 1918, a civil war began in Russia. The forces that fought against the Communists became known as the White Army. After four years of fighting, however, the Communists defeated the White Army.

On December 28, 1922, the Communist government in Russia announced that it was joining with some lands that had one been part of the Russian Empire to create the Union of Soviet Socialist Republics, or Soviet Union. The Soviet Union soon began to expand, conquering and absorbing its neighbors in central Asia and eastern Europe. Like Russia before it, the Soviet Union was an empire.

As the country shifted to a Communist way of life, life became better for some Russians. But Russians did not have the freedom and equality that they had been promised. By switching to Communism, the Russian people had merely traded one type of harsh rule for another.

AMERICAN ACES JOIN THE AIR WAR

The airplane was still a new invention during the 1910s. Early planes were small and fragile. They were slow and needed two or three sets of wings to fly. Even so, the airplane became an important weapon during World War I.

At first, planes were used to spy on enemy ground troops. From the air, a pilot had a good view of the battlefield. He could see where enemy soldiers were hiding. He could also warn his side of an enemy attack. Soon there were many planes in the air. When a pilot came across an enemy airplane, he fired at it with a pistol or shotgun. After a while, each side began mounting machine guns on their airplanes. This made it possible for pilots to shoot each other down. A pilot who shot down five enemy planes was called an ace.

During World War I, aerial combat became known as "dogfighting." People on the ground said that during battles, the early airplanes' engines sometimes sounded like dogs barking.

Baron Manfred von Richthofen (1892–1918), the Red Baron, received his nickname because he preferred his airplanes to be painted bright red.

Eddie Rickenbacker (1890–1973) was the leading American ace. He shot down twenty-six enemy aircraft.

The first air aces were German, French, and British. Germany's Manfred von Richthofen was nicknamed the Red Baron. He scored eighty victories before he was shot down in April 1918. America's top ace was Eddie Rickenbacker. He had been a racecar driver before the war. Rickenbacker shot down dozens of enemy aircraft. He received the Congressional Medal of Honor for his heroics.

During World War I, the U.S. Army was in charge of military aircraft. Posters like these were used to attract new recruits to the Army Air Service.

JOIN THE ARMY AIR SERVICE BE AN AMERICAN EAGLE!

CONSULT YOUR LOCAL DRAFT BOARD, READ THE ILLUSTRATED BOOKLET AT ANY RECRUITING OFFICE, OR WRITE TO THE CHIEF SIGNAL OFFICER OF THE ARMY, WASHINGTON. D. C.

SPORTS IN THE 1910s

The war affected all parts of life, including sports. The 1916 Summer Olympics were originally scheduled to take place in Berlin, Germany. At first, people thought the war would be over by then. As the fighting raged on, it became clear that the war would continue through 1916. The Olympics were cancelled.

Americans could still forget about the war by enjoying baseball, a very popular sport in America's growing cities. However, a cheating scandal

A baseball card from 1911 shows a player sliding safely into third base. By the 1910s, baseball was the most popular sport in America. The decade 1910–1919 saw the construction of many ballparks that could hold large crowds. Two are still in use today: Fenway Park in Boston (built in 1912) and Wrigley Field in Chicago (built in 1914).

A *New York Times* story describes the so-called "Black Sox" scandal of 1919. Pitcher Eddie Cicotte and left fielder "Shoeless" Joe Jackson, mentioned in the headline, were two of major league baseball's best players.

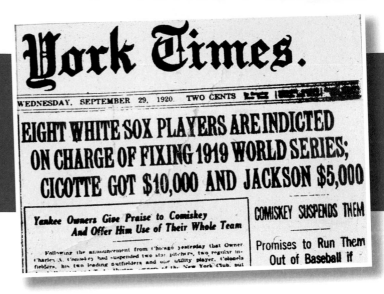

York Times.

WEDNESDAY, SEPTEMBER 29, 1920   TWO CENTS

EIGHT WHITE SOX PLAYERS ARE INDICTED ON CHARGE OF FIXING 1919 WORLD SERIES; CICOTTE GOT $10,000 AND JACKSON $5,000

Yankee Owners Give Praise to Comiskey And Offer Him Use of Their Whole Team

Following the announcement from Chicago yesterday that Owner Charles A. Comiskey had suspended two star pitchers, two regular infielders, his two leading outfielders and one utility player. Colonels

COMISKEY SUSPENDS THEM

Promises to Run Them Out of Baseball if

rocked that sport in 1919. Seven players from the Chicago White Sox secretly accepted money to lose the World Series on purpose. The guilty players, along with another player who had refused to take part in the fix but did not tell the authorities beforehand, were banned from the major leagues for life. Disgusted fans called the team the Black Sox.

Boxing was very popular in the 1910s. Jack Dempsey was a beloved boxer. As a youth, he earned a living by boxing for money in taverns or small clubs. Dempsey then became a professional fighter. He amazed fans with his strength and his ability to take punches without being knocked down. In 1918, he won an amazing fifteen bouts and lost just one. A year later, Jack Dempsey captured the world heavyweight championship. He would defend the title many times.

Jess Willard sits up after being knocked to the canvas by Jack Dempsey during their world heavyweight title fight on July 4, 1919. Dempsey won the fight at the end of the third round. He held the heavyweight title until 1926.

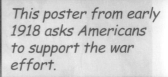
This poster from early 1918 asks Americans to support the war effort.

JOSEPH PENNELL DEL.

THAT LIBERTY SHALL NOT PERISH FROM THE EARTH BUY LIBERTY BONDS
FOURTH LIBERTY LOAN

PRESIDENT WILSON PROPOSES PEACE

By 1918, the Allies were slowly winning the war. Germany was losing, but far from beaten. Millions of soldiers were already dead or wounded. Many more would surely die in the battles that lay ahead. The world was tired of this brutal war. People in Europe and America wanted it to end. As the fighting continued, President Woodrow Wilson stepped forward with a plan for peace.

Wilson's plan was called the Fourteen Points. It contained fourteen key ideas for peace. President Wilson made a speech before Congress about it on January 8, 1918. He said that nations needed to work together for peace.

General John J. Pershing (1860–1948) was the U.S. commander in France. His army was called the American Expeditionary Force. Most American soldiers did not arrive in Europe until the spring of 1918. As the American Expeditionary Force grew larger, it began to turn the tide of the war against Germany.

African Americans overcame racial discrimination to make important contributions to American success in World War I. These soldiers are members of the 369th Infantry Regiment. Members of this unit, which was composed entirely of African-American soldiers, earned many medals for their service. The entire regiment was awarded the Croix de Guerre, France's highest military honor, for its part in a 1918 battle.

He did not like what had happened in Europe before the war. Nations had built huge armies and huge empires. They had engaged in secret talks. They had threatened each other. The president felt that these acts had led to war.

Wilson wanted freedom and cooperation. He said that the seas of the world should be open to all nations. Each country should agree to limit the size of its army and navy. They should trade with each other fairly and honorably. Most importantly, Wilson thought that countries should discuss matters openly. For this purpose, he suggested an international organization of countries. Wilson's proposed League of Nations would be a place where diplomats from member nations could meet. They would talk about the world's problems and try to find peaceful solutions. In this way, President Wilson felt that future wars could be avoided. Wilson would have to wait until the war ended, however, to see whether both sides would accept these Fourteen Points.

WOODROW WILSON: PRESIDENT AND SCHOLAR

Thomas Woodrow Wilson was born into a minister's family in 1856. He knew the value of hard work and study. Young Wilson went to Princeton University and two other schools. He then embarked on a career of teaching and writing.

Wilson later returned to Princeton as a professor. He went on to become the school's president. In 1910, he ran for governor of New Jersey and won. Voters liked his honesty and dedication to progressivism and reform. Two years later, in 1912, Woodrow Wilson was elected the twenty-eighth president of the United States. During the 1912 election, Theodore Roosevelt split the Republican vote with William Taft, allowing the Democratic candidate, Wilson, to win.

Wilson was re-elected in 1916, in part because he had kept America out of World War I. However, in April 1917, the president would lead America into the conflict that he hoped would prevent future wars. For his role in ending World War I, Wilson received the 1919 Nobel Peace Prize. Woodrow Wilson died in 1924.

Some historians believe that Woodrow Wilson was one of the greatest American presidents.

First Woman Elected to Congress

Women made great strides during the 1910s. In 1916, Jeannette Rankin became the first woman elected to the U.S. Congress. At the time, laws barred women from voting in many elections in the United States. Rankin hoped to help change that.

The right to vote is called suffrage. A suffragist is someone who supported the right of women to vote. There are many famous suffragists in American history. Elizabeth Cady Stanton and Susan B. Anthony are two examples. During the 1800s, they fought for women's right

Jeannette Rankin (1880–1973) served two terms in the U.S. House of Representatives (1917–1919 and 1941–1943). Throughout her political career she supported programs to help women and children. She also helped to establish the American Civil Liberties Union. This group, which is still active today, works to defend and preserve the individual rights and liberties guaranteed to all American citizens by the Constitution and national laws.

This cartoon from 1914 depicts a farmer speaking with five suffragettes who are marching down a country road with a banner that says "Votes for Women."

to vote. Slowly, the suffragists made progress. By the 1910s, some states, such as Colorado, Idaho, Utah, and Wyoming, allowed women to vote in certain elections. However, most women still could not vote for president of the United States.

Jeannette Rankin was born in Montana in 1880. As a young woman, she attended college. Later, she fought for women's suffrage in Montana and the state of Washington. Rankin wanted to prove that a woman could also hold political office. She ran for the U.S. House of Representatives in 1916. The voters of Montana elected her. In Congress, Rankin helped write new health-care laws. Many of her efforts aimed to improve health care for children and mothers. She also opposed U.S. involvement in World War I.

Women demonstrate outside the White House holding suffrage banners, 1917. One reads, "Mr President, How Long Must Women Wait For Liberty?" The demonstrators were members of a group called the Silent Sentinels. They picketed in Washington, D.C., from 1917 until June 1919, when Congress passed the Nineteenth Amendment to the U.S. Constitution. That amendment, which gave women the right to vote, was ratified in 1920.

New Authors, New Ideas

Long before television and the Internet, people looked to books for entertainment. A good novel was always in demand. During the 1910s, some creative authors invented new ways to tell a story. They were known as the modernists. There were modernists in many other forms of art, architecture, literature, and music.

James Joyce was an Irish author. He was one of the first modernists. His books did more than simply describe people, places, and things. Joyce wanted readers to know the views and feelings of the people in his books. So he told his stories by writing down their thoughts. Readers could

James Joyce (1882–1941) was born in Ireland, but he moved throughout Europe in the early years of the twentieth century. He gained literary fame in 1914 with the publication of *Dubliners*, a book of short stories. He followed this success with the acclaimed novels *A Portrait of the Artist as a Young Man* (1916), *Ulysses* (1922), and *Finnegan's Wake* (1939).

The English writer Virginia Woolf (1882–1941) is considered one of the most important figures in the modernist literary movement. She is best known for her novels *Mrs. Dalloway* (1925) and *To the Lighthouse* (1927), as well as her long essay *A Room of One's Own* (1929).

see what the story's characters were thinking. It was a unique approach. One of Joyce's most famous novels was *A Portrait of the Artist as a Young Man*, published in 1916. A later novel, *Ulysses*, is considered one of the finest books ever written.

Like Joyce, British writer Virginia Woolf was a modernist. Her books also explored inner thoughts and feelings. She liked to show how each person might react differently to the same event. Woolf's first novel was called *The Voyage Out*. It was first published in 1915. She wrote many other popular books afterward.

During the 1910s, Nebraska-born author Willa Cather (1873–1947) wrote four best-selling novels. Many of her works are about life on the American prairies of the Midwest. *My Ántonia*, published in 1918, is considered her finest work.

Deadly Flu
Kills Millions

Influenza is a common illness. Most people know it as the flu. It comes from a virus. Usually, a person with the flu starts to feel better after a few days. However, in 1918, a deadly type of flu began to spread.

Nobody knows for sure where the deadly flu started. Newspaper reporters first learned of it in Spain. They named it the Spanish flu. World War I helped the virus spread quickly. Soldiers traveling to and from the war unknowingly carried the virus with them.

Once infected, people usually became too weak to walk within hours. Some eventually got better, but many died. Unlike most types of influenza, the

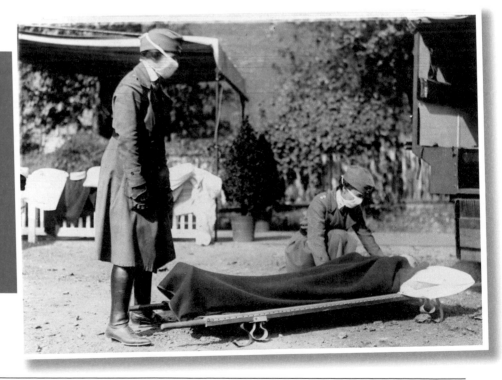

American Red Cross volunteers care for a sick person at an emergency medical station in Washington, D.C., during the influenza pandemic of 1918.

Local health departments warned people who were ill to stay away from theaters and other public places.

Spanish flu was hardest on adults. Most of its victims were between the ages of twenty and forty.

The total death count around the world was more than 50 million people—more than had died in World War I. More than six hundred thousand Americans died of the flu, far more than had died in combat. People were afraid to go to school or work. They stayed indoors so they would not get sick. However, the Spanish flu vanished in 1919 almost as quickly as it came.

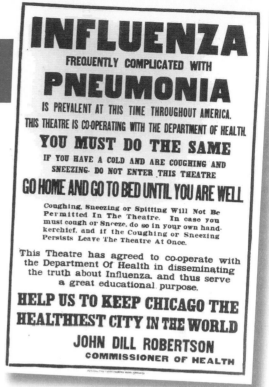

INFLUENZA
FREQUENTLY COMPLICATED WITH
PNEUMONIA
IS PREVALENT AT THIS TIME THROUGHOUT AMERICA.
THIS THEATRE IS CO-OPERATING WITH THE DEPARTMENT OF HEALTH.
YOU MUST DO THE SAME
IF YOU HAVE A COLD AND ARE COUGHING AND SNEEZING. DO NOT ENTER THIS THEATRE
GO HOME AND GO TO BED UNTIL YOU ARE WELL
Coughing, Sneezing or Spitting Will Not Be Permitted In The Theatre. In case you must cough or Sneeze, do so in your own handkerchief, and if the Coughing or Sneezing Persists Leave The Theatre At Once.
This Theatre has agreed to co-operate with the Department Of Health in disseminating the truth about Influenza, and thus serve a great educational purpose.
HELP US TO KEEP CHICAGO THE HEALTHIEST CITY IN THE WORLD
JOHN DILL ROBERTSON
COMMISSIONER OF HEALTH

Large buildings, such as this auditorium in Iowa, were often used as makeshift hospitals. The doctors and nurses pictured in this photo are wearing cloth masks. People believed the masks would protect them from the influenza virus. However, the masks provided very little protection.

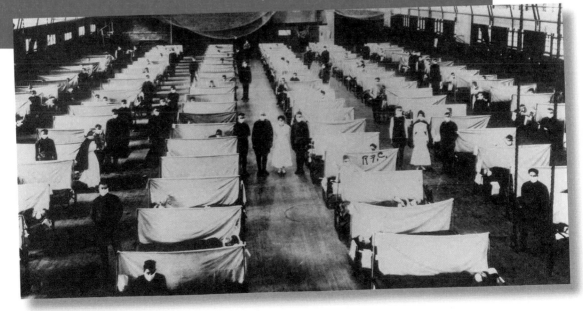

German diplomats sign the Peace Treaty of Versailles on June 28, 1919.

Treaty of Versailles Brings an Uneasy Peace

By the fall of 1918, Germany's leaders realized that they could not win the war. Rather than let the bloodshed continue, they wanted peace. An armistice—which means that both sides agreed to stop fighting and to negotiate a peace treaty—went into effect on November 11, 1918, at 11 A.M. It was the eleventh hour of the eleventh day of the eleventh month of the year.

People in New York's Times Square celebrate a news report that Germany had signed an armistice, ending the fighting in World War I, November 1918.

The leaders of the major Allied powers were known as the "Big Four." They were (left to right) David Lloyd George of Great Britain, Orlando Vittorio of Italy, Georges Clemenceau of France, and U.S. president Woodrow Wilson. The Big Four oversaw a peace conference in Paris that lasted for six months. During that time, they broke up the Austro-Hungarian and Ottoman empires, created many new countries, and pondered the fate of Germany.

With the truce in place, leaders of the Allies gathered at Versailles, a palace near the French capital, Paris. They discussed the terms under which they would accept Germany's surrender. England and France had very harsh demands. They wanted to break up the Austro-Hungarian and Ottoman empires completely. They wanted to limit the size of the German military and force Germany to give up its overseas colonies. They also wanted Germany to pay for the war.

U.S. President Woodrow Wilson disliked the greedy nature of the conference. He wished to create a fair settlement for all nations. He felt that fairness would lead to a lasting peace. However, his European allies seemed interested only in punishing Germany and taking its riches. One by one, Wilson's Fourteen Points were tossed aside. Desperately, Wilson clung to his most important idea—the League of Nations. President Wilson made many compromises in order to keep his dream alive.

When the German delegates arrived in Versailles, they were shocked. The treaty before them was nothing like the Fourteen Points. It would place a heavy burden on their nation. The Germans protested the treaty as unfair. However, Germany was unable to fight any longer. Its leaders had to accept the terms of the treaty. They signed it on June 28, 1919. The Great War was officially over.

The Treaty of Versailles angered the German people. They did not believe that their nation had really lost the war. No foreign soldier had even set foot on German soil. The Germans also refused to accept blame for starting the war.

The debt Germany owed to the Allies totaled tens of billions of dollars. It was paid in German ships, trains, money, and natural resources. For years, these debt payments took resources away from German businesses and government. Factories and other businesses closed, and many people lost their jobs. The nation's economy was crippled. The misery and bitterness of the post-war period would help Adolf Hitler and his Nazi Party take control of Germany during the 1930s.

German soldiers destroy rifles as required by the Treaty of Versailles. The peace agreement forced Germany to scrap most of its weapons and reduce the size of its army.

Congress Rejects the League of Nations

President Woodrow Wilson's problems continued at home. The League of Nations was his creation. He had argued tirelessly for it in Europe. However, upon returning to the United States, he learned that his own nation was against the idea.

Many Americans were unhappy with the outcome of the war. The Allies had won, but it felt like an empty victory. U.S. soldiers had fought and died, but most Americans still did not understand why. It seemed that the countries of Europe had started the war only to broaden their empires. Americans thought that if they joined the League of Nations, one day the United States might be forced to fight another European war. As a result, many Americans were against joining the League.

President Wilson tried to convince people that membership was a good idea. He traveled the country. He explained how the League could help prevent another war. Wilson's pleas were unsuccessful. People remained

This April 1920 cartoon from the *Chicago Tribune* reflects American attitudes toward the League of Nations. It criticizes four leading members of the League (France, Britain, Italy, and Japan) for failing to promote world peace. Instead, they are depicted sowing the seeds of war.

U.S. Senator Henry Cabot Lodge (1850–1924) led the fight against America's joining the League of Nations. For most of America's history, the country had tried to stay out of other countries' affairs. Lodge wanted a return to this isolationist position. He did not want the United States to become entangled in European problems after World War I.

cautious about involvement with foreign countries. In September 1919, President Wilson suffered a stroke. He could no longer make public speeches. Two months later, the U.S. Senate rejected membership in the League of Nations.

The countries that did join tried to make the League of Nations successful. They found it difficult to do so. However, the League of Nations proved to be a small step toward world peace. It would help inspire the creation of the far more successful United Nations in 1945.

This palace in Geneva, Switzerland, once served as headquarters for the League of Nations. Although the League had been formed to help prevent warfare, it had to depend on the Great Powers to enforce its resolutions. After World War I, however, many countries were reluctant to take military action. As a result, during the 1930s, the League was unable to prevent Japan, Italy, and Germany from attacking other countries.

Looking Ahead

The decade 1910–1919 was filled with tragedy and sorrow. World War I and the deadly influenza pandemic had combined to kill tens of millions of people by the end of the decade. By 1920, those who had survived these tragedies were ready to have some fun. A new era known as the "Roaring Twenties" soon began in the United States.

The 1920s were a time of many social changes in America. Women gained the right to vote in national elections. Young women, who became known as "flappers," began to wear bold clothing in public. Immigrants and African Americans also sought greater rights as American citizens.

During the 1920s, it was illegal to manufacture, sell, or transport alcoholic beverages. This period became known as Prohibition. Laws banning alcohol had been passed to reduce crime, but they had the opposite effect. Americans continued to drink alcohol during Prohibition, and gangsters became wealthy by smuggling and selling illegal liquor.

The decade was also known for consumer spending. Factories turned out many new products, such as washing machines and radios. People borrowed money to purchase these products. They also invested their savings in the stock market. The wild spending hid problems in the American economy. The decade closed with a terrible stock market collapse in October 1929. The world soon found itself mired in the Great Depression.

A liquor agent destroys kegs of illegal beer, 1924. In 1920 it became illegal to manufacture, sell, or transport alcoholic beverages in the United States. Despite the new laws, many Americans continued to drink alcohol secretly during the Prohibition period.

CHRONOLOGY

1910—Japan makes Korea part of its territory in August. The Mexican Revolution begins. In America, the Boy Scouts are founded.

1911—The Republic of China is established.

1912—The Girl Scouts of the United States of America are founded in March. *Titanic* sinks on April 15. Theodore Roosevelt forms the Progressive, or Bull Moose, Party. Woodrow Wilson is elected president.

1913—The Sixteenth Amendment to the Constitution is ratified. It enables the federal government to collect income tax.

1914—The Panama Canal officially opens. Archduke Franz Ferdinand of Austria is killed in June. World War I begins less than two months later.

1915—A German U-boat sinks the *Lusitania* in May. Among the victims are 128 Americans.

1916—U.S. forces pursue Pancho Villa in Mexico. Jeannette Rankin becomes the first woman elected to Congress.

1917—America enters World War I in April. The Russian Revolution leads to a civil war between Communist and non-Communist forces.

1918—Woodrow Wilson proposes his Fourteen Points for peace in January. The Spanish flu appears in August. A November 11 armistice ends the fighting in Europe.

1919—The Treaty of Versailles is signed in June. The League of Nations is created. The United States refuses to join the League in November.

 Glossary

alliance—A collection of nations or groups working toward a common goal.

ambassador—A person who officially represents a country; a diplomat.

armistice—An agreement to stop fighting.

candidate—A person who is seeking public office.

colony—A territory owned or controlled by a distant country.

dogfighting—In war, combat between airplanes.

empire—A powerful nation that controls a great deal of territory, including lands that have been conquered or colonized by military force.

improvisation—An unplanned change, invention, or creation.

influenza—A viral disease that causes fever, chills, and breathing problems; the flu.

scandal—A disgraceful incident.

stroke—A loss of brain function due to a blockage or disturbance in the blood vessels that supply blood to the brain.

virus—A tiny particle that lives within a host, such as a person or animal. Viruses often reproduce within the host, and this can cause illness.

FURTHER READING

Bobek, Milan, editor. *Decades of the Twentieth Century: The 1910s*. Pittsburgh, Pa.: Eldorado Ink, 2005.

Caper, William. *Nightmare on the Titanic*. New York: Bearport Publishing, 2007.

Englar, Mary. *Pancho Villa: Rebel of the Mexican Revolution*. Bloomington, Minn.: Capstone Press, 2006.

Gavin, Lettie. *American Women in World War I: They Also Served*. Boulder, Colo.: University Press of Colorado, 2006.

Hagedorn, Ann. *Savage Peace: Hope and Fear in America, 1919*. New York: Simon and Schuster, 2007.

Hammerschmidt, Peter. *History of American Immigration*. Philadelphia: Mason Crest, 2008.

Krohn, Katherine. *The 1918 Flu Pandemic*. Illus. by Bob Hall, Keith Williams, and Charles Barnett III. Bloomington, Minn.: Capstone Press, 2007.

Lukes, Bonnie. *Woodrow Wilson and the Progressive Era*. Greensboro, N.C.: Morgan Reynolds, 2005.

Meachen Rau, Dana. *Great Women of the Suffrage Movement*. Mankato, Minn.: Compass Point Books, 2006.

Woelfle, Gretchen. *Jeannette Rankin: Political Pioneer*. Honesdale, Pa.: Calkins Creek Books, 2007.

INTERNET RESOURCES

<http://magma.nationalgeographic.com/ngexplorer/0411/articles/mainarticle.html>
This Web site for young adults provides information about the famous ocean liner *Titanic*, including photos of the sunken wreck today.

<http://www.pbs.org/greatwar/>
An interesting study of World War I. It describes the war's impact on the course of history.

<http://nobelprize.org/nobel_prizes/peace/laureates/1919/wilson-bio.html>
The Nobel Foundation's profile of its 1919 Peace Prize recipient, U.S. president Woodrow Wilson.

INDEX

Italy, 22, 52, 54, 55

Jackson, Joe ("Shoeless"), 39
Japan, 15, 22, 54, 55
jazz music, 28–29
  See also entertainment
Joyce, James, 46–47

Kennedy, John F., 12

League of Nations, 43, 53,
  54–55
Lenin, Vladimir, 34, 35
Liberty Bonds, 13, 40
Lloyd George, David, 52
Lodge, Henry Cabot, 55
Low, Juliette Gordon, 13
Lusitania, 24, 25

MacArthur, Douglas, 27
medicine
  flu epidemic, 6, 48–49, 56
Mexico, 26–27, 30, 31
modernism, 46–47
Montenegro, 22
movies, 7, 18–19
  See also entertainment
Mrs. Dalloway (Woolf), 47
music, 28–29
  See also entertainment
My Ántonia (Cather), 47

New Mexico, 17, 26, 30
New York Herald, 10
New York Times, 39
Nicholas II (Tsar), 32, 33, 34
Nineteenth Amendment, 45

Olympics, 38
Ottoman Empire, 21, 22, 52

Patton, George S., 27
Pershing, John J., 27, 41
Pickford, Mary, 19

Porter, Edwin, 18
*A Portrait of the Artist as a
  Young Man* (Joyce), 46, 47
progressivism, 6, 7, 43
Prohibition, 56–57
"Punitive Expedition," 26,
  27

Rankin, Jeannette, 44, 45
Richthofen, Manfred von
  (Red Baron), 36, 37
Rickenbacker, Eddie, 37
A Room of One's Own
  (Woolf), 47
Roosevelt, Theodore, 43
Russia, 6, 21, 22
  revolution in, 32–35

Scouting for Boys (Baden-
  Powell), 13
Serbia, 21–22
Seton, Ernest Thompson, 13
Seventeenth Amendment, 7
Silent Sentinels, 45
Sixteenth Amendment, 16,
  17
Sons of Daniel Boone, 13
Soviet Union, 34, 35
  See also Russia
Spanish flu. *See* flu epidemic
sports, 38–39
Stanton, Elizabeth Cady, 44
Stead, William T., 10
Straus, Isidor, 10
submarines, 6, 25, 30, 31
suffrage, 7, 44–45, 56

Taft, William Howard, 16, 43
tariffs, 17
taxes, 16–17
technology
  airplanes, 36–37
  weapons, 6, 23
Three Friends (movie), 19

Titanic, 5–6, 8–11
To the Lighthouse (Woolf), 47
Treaty of Versailles, 50,
  52–53
  See also World War I
Trotsky, Leon, 34

Ulysses (Joyce), 46, 47
United Nations, 55

Villa, Francisco ("Pancho"),
  26–27
Vittorio, Orlando, 52
voting rights, 7, 44–45, 56
The Voyage Out (Woolf), 47

weapons, 6, 23
White Army, 34, 35
Wilhelm II, 21
Willard, Jess, 39
Wilson, Woodrow, 7, 24, 25,
  27, 30–31, 54–55
  and the Fourteen Points,
    41–43, 52–53
  women's rights, 7, 44–45, 56
Woodland Scouts, 13
Woolf, Virginia, 47
World Series scandal, 38–39
World War I, 5, 6–7, 13, 38, 56
  and aerial combat, 36–36
  and American neutrality,
    24–25, 30–31
  America's involvement in,
    31, 40–43
  causes of, 21–23
  end of, 51–53
  Russian involvement in,
    33, 34, 35
  and Spanish flu, 48

Zimmerman, Arthur, 30
"Zimmerman Telegram,"
  30, 31
See also World War I

Picture Credits

Illustration credits: Bildarchiv Preussischer Kulturbesitz/Art Resource, NY: 50; Erich Lessing/Art Resource, NY: 36 (top); Press Association via AP Images: 9; Duke University: 5; © Yann Forget: 55 (bottom); Getty Images: 33, 39, 43, 53; Popperfoto/Getty Images: 23 (top); Time and Life Pictures/Getty Images: 41; The Granger Collection, New York: 17 (bottom), 46, 47, 54, 57; © 2009 Jupiterimages Corporation: 1 (Bottom), 8, 12 (top), 32; Library of Congress: 4, 6, 7, 10, 12 (bottom), 13, 14 (top), 15, 16, 18, 19 (top), 20, 24, 25 (bottom), 29, 31 (bottom), 37 (bottom), 38, 40, 44, 45, 48, 55 (top); National Archives and Records Administration: 1 (top left), 17 (top), 23 (bottom), 25 (top), 26, 27, 30, 31 (top), 36 (bottom), 37 (top), 42, 51, 52; NOAA/Institute for Exploration/University of Rhode Island: 11; Office of the Public Health Service Historian: 1 (top right), 49; © 2009 OTTN Publishing: 22; used under license from Shutterstock, Inc.: 14 (bottom), 19 (bottom), 28, 34, 35.

Cover photos: National Archives and Records Administration (soldiers in trench); Office of the Public Health Service Historian (Influenza Pandemic), © 2009 Jupiterimages Corporation (Titanic sinking).